A COUGAR'S GUIDE TO GETTING YOUR ASS BACK OUT THERE

....

KARENLEE POTER

LoveEncore, LLC
P.O. Box 601
Northbrook, IL 60062
www.karenleepotershow.com

Publisher's Note: This is a work of fiction. Names, characters, places, and incidents are a product of the author's imagination. Locales and public names are sometimes used for atmospheric purposes. Any resemblance to actual people, living or dead, or to businesses, companies, events, institutions, or locales is completely coincidental.

Book Layout ©2013 BookDesignTemplates.com
A Cougar's Guide To Getting Your Ass Back Out There Karen-Lee Poter.

1st ed.ISBN 978-0-692-46781-7

THIS BOOK IS DEDICATED TO MY
CHILDREN: JESSICA,
CAMERON, & JEREMY

AND THE TWO LOVES OF MY
LIFE: GARY & STEVE

·······································

AGING IS NOT LOST YOUTH BUT
A NEW STAGE OF OPPORTUNITY
AND STRENGTH.

-BETTY FRIEDAN

TABLE OF CONTENTS

....

ACKNOWLEDGMENTS

....

This book was in the works for several years but would not have been written without the encouragement and brilliant editing skills of one of my best friends, Wendy Frink. Thanks for your love and friendship. I'd also like to thank Julie Holloway for coming through in the clutch when I needed emergency book formatting help. An additional thank you goes to my gifted daughter Jessica. Your attention to detail and help pulling it all together put the finishing touches on this baby. I love you, Belle! Last but not least, I must thank the person who inspired me to write this book, Steve Koenig. I couldn't have done it without your love, support, and unwavering commitment. I am one lucky woman to have you all in my life.

INTRODUCTION

....

A Cougar's Guide To Getting Your Ass Back Out There? You're probably scratching your head trying to register what this title means. The word "Cougar" has such a negative connotation; why on earth would someone want to put it in the title of a self-help book? What kind of lunatic would want to be called a Cougar? Who would take advice from me, a prowling predator of innocent younger men?

Before you slam the book shut, give me a chance to explain. Cougar is a term that I've come to embrace. There's no other word in the English language that describes a woman who is confident, older, unique, genuine, assertive and racy like the word COUGAR. I've wracked my brain trying to come up with a better word to no avail. I've decided to embrace the term. I challenge you to awaken your inner COUGAR!

Why did I write this book? Eight years ago my husband was murdered, and I found myself suddenly single after being married for 24 years. I had no idea what I was supposed to do with my life. I had not utilized my master's degree in social work since the mid 80's. At the time, I was a stay-at-home mom with a part-time video editing business.

My life had turned upside down, and I decided to go out into the dating world. I was shocked at what I found and how little I was prepared for this game-changer. I read blogs and books, talked to widows and divorcees, and watched YouTube videos trying to get information on navigating the singles world later in life. I found that experience was the best teacher.

Two years ago, I created a forum for discussion on my YouTube channel: The KarenLee Poter Show. My show, which has received well over a million views, has become my passion. Because there are many that prefer the written word, I felt compelled to write this book from the perspective of a proud Cougar. I divided it into two parts: redefining the word "Cougar" and getting your ass back out there. As Helen Reddy said, "I am woman, hear me roar."

PART ONE

···

GETTING YOUR ASS BACK OUT THERE

ONE

....

SHY TO BOLD: METAMORPHOSIS

Experience is the teacher of all things.

-JULIUS CAESAR

I wasn't always an outgoing, confident Cougar. In fact, I was the antithesis of one. I would classify myself as more of a timid, insecure rabbit. I was a shy, docile toddler, the kind that allowed her pail and shovel to be grabbed from her in the sandbox on a daily basis.

Here's another example of my timidity; my mom had to call my pre-school after I came home and announced that my part in the school Purim play was "the audience." That year there were two Queen Esthers.

Around 12 years old, I became a little boy-crazy, a theme that appears in multiple entries of my diary:

"Today was the boy-girl party. All the boys liked me the best. At least most did. I kissed Larry on the lips!" and "Today I pulled Billy's zipper and everyone was going, 'Oh oh, now we know.' And Billy said, 'I enjoyed it all.'"

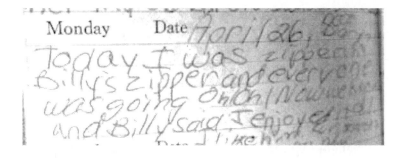

Being the eldest child in my family, I was a few steps behind many of my peers in my sexual maturation. I had no older siblings to show me the ropes. I was extremely naive about my body and sexuality. I went through puberty really late and entered high school completely paranoid about my lack of boobs.

One of the most embarrassing moments of my life occurred in the high school cafeteria at the end of my freshman year. I was sitting with a small group, when all of a sudden a boy decided to run up to me, bite one of my nonexistent breasts, and run the other way. The entire cafeteria burst into gales of laughter, and I was so humiliated I  wanted to hide under the table. Unfortunately, my extremely flat size A cups developed overnight to a whopping D. I became even more self-conscious and thought I was too big.

Here's my journal entry at age 15:
"I was looking through my cabinet and came across this. I found that my mind has matured so much but the basic principles are still the same. I matured late and that affected my personality. I felt inferior also. I'm still changing and maybe someday I'll look back at this and laugh but until then BYE! Luv, Karen"

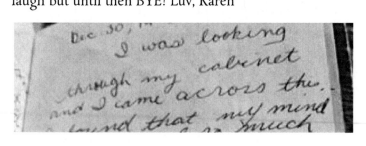

Lucky for me, I do look back and laugh at that shy young girl who ultimately turned into the confident independent woman that I am today.

There were several boys who impacted my confidence level during high school.

I went out with one boy named Bruce mainly because he was able to drive his dad's lime green Cadillac and took me to movies and dinners. I was enjoying the attention until he decided to add up how much money he'd spent on me. I took offense to this, and that was the end of Bruce. No one would accuse me of being a gold digger, even though that green Caddie was "out of sight." There was Ron, who had long dirty blond hair and played guitar in the park. We made out in the rain, and those memories still get my juices flowing. During my junior year, I had an intense crush on a senior named Bill. He was  the president of the student council, and I joined just to be near him. He flirted, I fawned, and every other day, I came home with a new story to tell my mom about Bill and how he promised to take me to the prom. I blindly believed him and couldn't wait until it happened.

When he asked Caroline instead, I came home and cried to my mother. It sounds like fairly typical high school drama, but it was my obsession for that time period. I must say that karma is a bitch, and when he asked me out in college, I seized the opportunity to sexually tease him and then blow him off.

Decades later, I heard he nearly went to prison for fraud, so I'm glad my intuition led me in the right direction - away from him! I had a "nice" relationship with a guy named Tommy who went to Northwestern University during my senior year of high school. I was proud to be taking a college boy to my prom, but that night I should've won an award for the biggest teenage cocktease.

Here's what happened: Tommy and I were on the couch dry humping and making out.

Me: Tommy, do you want to have sex?

Tommy: Yes.

Me: Well I'm not ready.

The Cougar side of me lay very dormant during this time of my life. Although I was a late-bloomer, I managed to make up for it in college. Since I was the eldest of three kids, I had to do a lot of ice breaking. My parents decided to give me a 12 o'clock curfew the summer before my freshman year at the University of Illinois – so when I got to Champaign, I stayed up all night, just 'cause I could. I'll never forget the feeling of freedom from any parental restrictions that first year of college. I had the time of my life as I experimented with sex, drugs, and rock and roll. I had promised to stay "loyal" to my boyfriend, Tommy from home, but this lasted about one week. I looked around and saw the multitude of available guys and promptly sent him a "Dear John" letter. What was I thinking? I didn't have a boyfriend but experimented doing "everything but..." with several fraternity boys. I was pretty naive when it came to sex. It's amazing that I survived with some of the risky situations I put myself in. I had been saving my virginity for something special, which never materialized freshman year. One of my wilder sorority sisters gave me an ultimatum, "Don't come back from spring break unless you lose your virginity." I chose the boy who had pursued me for a year, whispering how much he wanted to be "The One," so I went back to his room and had a phenomenal time. This ended up being the best four years of my life!

I didn't have expectations that he'd be my future boy-friend, but I thought he would minimally have called me after my de-virginizing. Instead, I didn't hear from him until the following week. Did that stop me from doing it again? Hell no! At the time, I didn't feel manipulated and disrespected, but today I wouldn't put up with the kind of shenanigans that I allowed back then*.

*Although if he were super good in bed, I might be more forgiving.

I met my husband, Gary, during my sophomore year of college. I knew Gary was the guy I would marry. I've always been attracted to irreverent, funny, intelligent, trustworthy, handsome, kind, brave, thoughtful, loving, hardworking men. He fit the bill! Was it simple? No, in fact, I was "the other woman" while he dated another girl, Dena, who was quite straight-laced. I had been "friends" with him for a year until one night he impulsively kissed me. It took me by surprise when he said he'd wanted to do that for a long time.

This opened the gates to me seeing him every night behind his girlfriend's back. He would take Dena out, drop her off, and then pick me up to go back to his apartment. This was obviously during an un-Cougar-like period of my life. The sex was passionate and sneaking around added to the excitement. This lasted for about six months until I got fed up with being in the closet and not being the one going to the Spring Formal dances. I decided to draw a line in the sand - break up with Dena or we would be through. I was confident that he'd pick me and was shocked when he said he needed to stay with her because, "She needs me more."

I was being punished because I was a stronger girl! I

wasn't as needy and therefore, he should stay with her. That night I smoked a carton of Marlboro Lights and cried on his fraternity brother's shoulder. But it was the summer before my senior year, and I did manage to forget about Gary. I stayed in Champaign and took economics in summer school.

The first night there, I fell in lust with my next-door neighbor, Jimmy.

Jimmy was the polar opposite of Gary. He was from a small farm town; Gary was a city boy. Jimmy was muscular, blond, blue-eyed; and Gary was slender and dark. Gary was a quick-witted, fast-talking gambler, while

Jimmy was relaxed and let me run the show. After being with Jimmy for six months, I realized that although he was the perfect rebound guy, I had way too much control in our relationship and needed to move on.

Karma struck again, and Gary called to invite me to a wedding. I told him to take a hike! Of course, in true love story fashion, he persisted until I went for dinner with him. To assure me he was done with Dena, he burned a picture of her in the candle on our table. I entered graduate school in Champaign and drove back and forth to Chicago every weekend to stay with Gary in the house he rented with three other guys. It was like living in a fraternity, and I was the house mom. I loved every minute of it! I counseled the boys on their problems with women, and luxuriated in the attention I got for being the only girl. My self-confidence grew along with my love for Gary.

Upon graduating, I moved back home and continued to date Gary while working as a school social worker.

After dating exclusively for another year, at 21 years old, I succumbed to pressure from my parents and brought up the idea of marriage. We were married on July 4, 1982, at the ripe old age of 23, and I was happy to be Mrs. Gary Poter.

Our early years of marriage were filled with lots of lovemaking, fighting, laughter, more fighting, and fun.

We bought a condo in Glenview, a suburb of Chicago, and began our life together as a traditional husband and wife. It wasn't as much fun being a responsible married couple, but we traveled and enjoyed our time together. Gary wasn't a very verbally affectionate person, but would write the most beautifully worded cards on birthdays and holidays.

"If there's someone deserving of having a happy birthday, it's definitely you. You have worked so hard and long to be a great mom, companion, lover and friend. And now with the completion of our little family, life with you is wonderful – better than I'd ever imagined... I love you totally – today, tomorrow & forever."

Sex was always great, since Gary was innately a very generous lover. We both enjoyed all the spontaneous sex during those early years. He was actually more experimental than me – he liked to talk dirty, watch porn, and try new positions. Each Valentine's Day, he'd come home with a new sex toy or piece of sexy lingerie.

It wasn't all peaches and cream. We had some nasty squabbles, which once resulted in him giving me the silent treatment, and me pouring water on him while he was sleeping. We'd fight, have sex, make up - normal newlywed stuff. We decided to start a family and after a year of failed attempts, I went on fertility drugs. At age 27, I became pregnant and gave birth to my daughter, Jessica. I call the following eight years "the baby-making years," which lasted a very long time, since I had three late miscarriages, but joyfully resulted in giving birth to two sons.

These were the "mommy years," otherwise known as the "get away from me I want to sleep years."

No one tells you this, but when you're in "mommy mode," the last thing you want to do as you lay your head on your pillow is have someone tug at your pajamas and initiate sex. Gary was always ready for sex no matter how exhausted we both were, and it became an issue as the kids took up more of my waking hours. I didn't feel very Cougar-like as I immersed myself in the world of diapers, Tee-ball games, theater performances, and ballet recitals.

It got to a point when Gary threw out my favorite worn-out night shirt that read, "I can be very friendly," since he knew that wearing it meant I wasn't in the mood for sex. We finally came to a compromise, which was that Sunday night was our "sex night," and if I wanted sex on any other night I was to light a candle. Vacations were different, since without kids around, I was much more sexual.

I always enjoyed the sex but it wasn't a priority for me. My focus was directed solely towards my children and being a mom. I remember taking a nighttime class in astrology, and when the teacher asked if I'd like a private reading, I only asked him about my kids - nothing about myself.

I lived in a protective little suburban bubble without any aspirations other than being a wife and mother. I was blissfully happy during this phase of my life, but it wasn't about me. My Cougar spirit was nowhere to be found. I became a single woman after a phone call on the morning of May 16, 2006.

TWO

....

FROM MIXED COMPANY TO MURDER: HOW TRAGEDY BEGOT MY TRANSFORMATION

The truth is you don't know what is going to happen tomorrow. Life is a crazy ride, and nothing is guaranteed.

-EMINEM

Sometimes life hits you in the head with a brick. Don't lose faith.

-STEVE JOBS

I had been happily married to my college sweetheart, Gary, for nearly twenty-four years. We had a daughter and two sons who were 19, 17, and 11 years old.

I never dreamed a joyous musical rendezvous would precede a tragic event that would turn our wonderful world upside down...

My daughter, Jessica, had just finished her sophomore year at Yale University and had arranged for her a cappella group, Mixed Company, to perform in the Midwest area.

The group of 18 boys and girls would be staying at our house for the mid-May weekend and then drive up to Minnesota to finish the tour. On the Friday evening of their tour, we invited our friends and family to see them perform a show at one of our favorite restaurants, Café Lucci.

Nearly everyone we knew crammed into that room. (It was a magical night!) I remember glancing at Gary, who was grinning with pride as my daughter sang a solo. The rest of the weekend was filled with sightseeing and culminated with a private performance in our kitchen—a four-part harmony "Happy Mother's Day" song.

Gary joked on Monday night about how he was contemplating missing work the next day so he could drive to Minnesota with the group. Unfortunately, he did the responsible thing and went to work.

Tuesday morning, May 16, 2006, I received a frantic phone call from someone in Gary's office. Gary had been stabbed! I didn't know how badly he had been hurt, but I yelled for my daughter to come with me to the hospital. The boys were at school.

Gary was the president of a construction company. The previous day, he had given an employee, Tom, a pay cut during a routine job performance review.

Apparently, Tom wasn't happy about losing part of his income, and so he strolled into the office kitchen the next morning, slid a cake knife up his sleeve, casually said good morning to his colleagues, slinked into Gary's office, closed the door, plunged a knife into my husband's heart, and repeatedly stabbed him. He didn't stop until some co-workers stormed the office and pulled him off.

Jessica and I arrived at the hospital, and after a terrifying seclusion in a waiting room, we learned from a chaplain that Gary had died. Time froze as I looked at my daughter's face and the news sank in. My sister picked up my sons at school and told them about what had happened as she drove to the hospital.

That night, I made the determination that I wasn't going to be pitied and labeled as "the woman whose husband was murdered." I vowed that my kids would be strong, and our family would remain a family.

There isn't a day that goes by that I don't think about Gary. But I'm a much different person than I was back in 2006 when Mixed Company came to town. Gary's death was the launch pad for my transformation into a new life that I could hardly have imagined on the day that he was murdered.

I have learned a great deal about my capabilities as a person and navigator in the years since. Life's changes and the ways in which we handle them are what define us.

I want to share these experiences with The KarenLee Poter Show fans and hear the adventures of others who have likewise been transformed by their lives' events.

Photo of Gary and me taken the night of the event at Café Lucci.

THREE

....

OPEN YOUR WINDOW

A lot of people perceive women as sexy based on their outer appeal. But there's no way to mistake if a woman is confident.

-TREY SONGZ

There's always a window of opportunity, it's just whether you're ready to open it. I had been single for about a year and a half after my husband's sudden death. The first six months were devastating and filled with grief. Once the cloud of sadness began to lift, I embarked on my journey of finding my new self! I was still a mother, sister, daughter and friend, but I was no longer a wife. I found this to be scary yet liberating. I realized that dwelling on the past was a waste of time. Time took on a new meaning and importance.

Who was I? I had a need to discover my passions and improve the person who I had ignored for the past few decades by focusing on my family. I loved being a wife and full-time mother of three, but it was now MY time. I realized that going out to dinner with my married friends was comforting, but I needed more excitement. Trying to date the single men who I had known for years was not going to work. I was going to have to step out of my comfort zone and into the unknown single world.

I took an inventory of my mental and physical assets and deficits. I found that exercise helped me in both areas. Reading self-help books and seeing a therapist were both beneficial, but talking to other widows and divorcees was what I craved. They gave me tips from their years of dating as an older woman. I loved the attention I received when I went to singles bars. I felt like a teenager, with an added bonus, which was the experience I obtained from having been in a successful marriage. I loved myself and had been loved.

I ventured out with other single women and enjoyed the freedom that comes with being unattached. Meeting a whole new group of single women was an added benefit. I felt comfortable talking to guys as they approached me in restaurants or bars. I wasn't looking for my next husband. I was just out to have FUN and find a companion or two along the way. My secret to becoming this free-spirited woman can be summed up in one word: **C.O.U.G.A.R.** No, I wasn't looking to de-flower young innocent men as the stigma implied. I was evolving into that confident, older, unique, genuine, assertive and racy woman. Men seemed to be attracted to me because of the energy that I exuded. Did I dress sexy and youthful? Hell yes! Was I comfortable talking to men about any **spicy** subject? Of course! I decided that the race, religion or age of the men I met was not going to be a factor in my quest for companionship or future relationship. I didn't look for a man who fit societal norms. I was completely reliant on my intuition. This was very empowering. Were younger men attracted to the woman I had become? What do you think? A new Cougar had emerged.

PART TWO

···

REDEFINING THE C.O.U.G.A.R.

FOUR

....

SINGLE IS DIFFERENT THE SECOND TIME AROUND

Nobody grows old merely by living a number of years. We grow old by deserting our ideals. Years may wrinkle the skin, but to give up enthusiasm wrinkles the soul.

-SAMUEL ULLMAN

Close your eyes and recall your very first "official date."
Was it back in junior high school or after college? Visualize the total experience. Where did it take place? Were you excited to be with him/her or was it more of a

chance to try "dating"? Were you comfortable being with him or was it awkward? Did you have dates that turned into relationships or were you more of a serial dater?

Other than accepting a boy's I.D. bracelet in sixth grade, my first "official date" was in high school. The subsequent dates were more about the perks of dating versus boys that I enjoyed being with. These guys came with benefits such as: I'd have a date for the Homecoming Dance. Senior year I started dating a college guy. It held a lot of value until I left for college. Being free to date in college, experimenting sexually, and falling in love changed the landscape of dating for me. Meeting my husband and getting married right out of college, put an end to my dating... or did it?

Fast-forward your mental slideshow 10-30 years. Call to mind your first date as a widow or divorcee with kids and an ex-husband.

What was that first date like for you? Did you get fixed up, or did he ask you out after meeting you in a bar? Were you feeling the same awkwardness as you did back in high school? Was your confidence level the same or different dating this time around?

My lack of dating in my 20s and 30s had its pluses and minuses when it was time for me to get back out there. On one hand, I had plenty of self-confidence, not having experienced much rejection. On the other hand, I was naïve and therefore vulnerable - akin to a lamb going off to slaughter. I didn't know the little nuances of being single such as you don't have to talk to a boring stranger at a bar for an hour if he buys you a drink, or you don't have to give your phone number out just to be polite. Blind dates never made me nervous. I never worried that the guy wouldn't call me for a second date; rather, I worried as to how I could let him down without hurting his feelings. I wasn't in a hurry to find a "new husband" as much as I was interested in having some fun and companionship. Each one of us has a unique history of dating, both early on and after a relationship dissolves. It's up to us to remember this because all these past memories, thoughts and feelings have shaped us.

Recall the difficulties that occurred in your last relationship.

I'm sorry to tell you, but you played a part in those issues, and unless you realize what it was, it'll likely recur. There are always two sides to every story, find out what the other side to your story may have been by doing some self-reflecting and/or see a therapist.

Find out why you chose the person you married. Did you think he had problems that would change after you tied the knot? Did you see the red flags from day one? Were you a victim of someone with a shotgun forcing you to marry a crazy lunatic? Or did he just not meet your expectations? Looking back at your last marriage or relationship, did you "grow apart"? Focus on what you can do to make sure you "grow together" in the next relationship.

My husband loved to gamble and took a lot of risks. This was often reflected in his business decisions, online poker habit, and tendency to drive recklessly. Not long into our relationship, I realized that my current boyfriend had a similar behavior pattern. This was unsettling at first, until I realized I'm simply attracted to that type of guy. I had to make the choice to accept him the way he is, rather than fight to change it. As the Billy Joel song goes, "I love you just the way you are." Focus on changing what you can control – your reactions – rather than changing your partner's personality.

Close your eyes again – visualize what kind of person you want to be on a physical and mental level.
Are you that person? What can you do to become that image? One of my favorite Buddhist quotes is, "What you think, you become." Make it happen! Go to the gym, see a shrink, get a new job, style your hair, and/or join a charitable organization and make your vision a reality. It'll help your confidence level immensely. Men love confident, happy, and independent women. You'll have more power to choose the man rather than settling for who chooses you.

Create a mental list of people who can help spread the word that you're ready to date.
People are not mind readers. Don't assume that friends, co-workers, and family members know that you're ready to get back out there. They need to have

seeds planted that you're available, and it would be a good thing for them to fix you up with someone. I highly recommend that you try online dating or a dating service. You must find single friends of either sex to go out with. Don't shy away from going out alone to the local bar and making friends with the bartender. He can tell you who is single and who is married. He'll let you know the truth about the guys hitting on you. I've had a married man tell me he was single, only to be outed by the bartender. Like the Brownie Troop motto goes, making NEW single friends and keeping the OLD married ones is an essential part of being single and happy. You'll need to have a group of singles so if one's busy, there will be others to hang out with. The new friends can help you with your passions or careers and other aspects besides socializing. It's networking at its finest! I've connected with some fantastic women who've shared their friends with me. Forming new relationships with single people who've gone through similar life-altering circumstances can be comforting and enlightening. You can also meet new single friends through charity and religious organizations. Social media sites like Facebook are also great resources for making new connections.

Picture yourself on a date. What do you look like?

Would you run a marathon without getting in shape both physically and mentally? Of course not! If you're serious about finding a partner, you need to be prepared. Be confident about your physical appearance. Thankfully

Cougars aren't competing against 20-year-old bodies - your competition is other older women, fighting gravity and aging just like you.

Everyone has grey hairs and stretch marks. My friend Toni says, "Those are your natural tattoos." You need to choose to either do something about the extra flab around your waist or embrace it. If certain things like discolored teeth and a few wrinkles bother you, sell some stuff on ebay, get your teeth whitened, and treat yourself to a shot of Botox. It's worth it if it gives you confidence.

As far as your mental state, therapy is the best present you can give yourself. There are agencies that have sliding scales if cost is a deterrent. The other easy solution to feeling great mentally is getting your natural endorphins going with an exercise regimen. Find something you love doing: running, cycling, yoga or strength training, and put it into your week as a high priority. The endorphin rush will help revitalize you and put you in a great mood (at least for the 45 minutes after.) Use the Internet and watch videos on YouTube (here comes a plug) like TheKarenLee Poter Show. Go to the library, there are whole sections on self-help.

Envision signing a contract to never date a married man.

Make this a rule, and if you think you are vulnerable to falling for one, tell your friends and have them make you accountable. I have personally been victim to someone who said seven years ago that he was getting divorced and is still married today. Another married guy claimed to have been a widower, until a mutual friend told me that she was alive and kicking. Unfortunately the world is full of married men preying on single women. Here are some reasons why being with a married man is a no-win situation; you aren't a home wrecker, you wouldn't want that to happen to you, and he'll probably cheat on you, too. Once a dog always a dog. You have to be number one and have self-respect or no one will respect you.

Create a list of dos and don'ts on first dates. Here are some suggestions:

Do be honest, be yourself, and look happy. No matter how bad your day is going, turn it around and be positively radiant. If you don't think you look good, force a smile on your face. This will work wonders.

Do talk on the phone at least once before a date to make sure he's legit. Text conversations can be misleading.

Don't reveal too much about yourself before or on the first date.

Do think of it as fun and not as a job interview.

Don't be negative. Nobody wants to hear about the hostility you have for your ex-spouse/boyfriend.

Don't have sex on the first date, unless you're absolutely sure it's the right thing to do.

Do ask questions and listen to the answers. This will provide you with the information you need about his past and a possible future with you.

Don't drink too much.

Do use good table manners, yes it is common sense, but needs to be said.

Don't answer your cell phone unless it's a necessity – if you need to have it with you, put it on silent. No texting either, unless it's an emergency.

Do give good eye contact and warm body language.

Do offer to pay for the bill or at least split it. Do remember to thank the person for the date no matter how it turns out.

Do be polite to the waiter or bartender. Your date is watching you too.

Do be alert to RED flags on the first date. These are some actual statements - I kid you not:

> "I would only date someone who can help me pay my mortgage."
>
> "My ex is a c@*!t."
>
> "I'm not working right now because I'm waiting for my Dad to pass away, at which point I'll inherit a lot of money."

Do stay away from guys who have no boundaries on a first date. Such as the men who said:

> "I want to be upfront with you, I had prostrate cancer and if we have sex, you'll need to press a button on a penis pump that I wear."

"I won't be able to kiss you tonight because I have a giant canker sore in my mouth. I also am on medication for depression and anxiety."

Plan your *How Stella Got Her Groove Back* night ahead of time.

Only go to this step if you plan on being in a monogamous relationship. You deserve to be more than a one-night stand no matter how long it's been since you last had sex. Don't worry about being naked. Your partner will be naked too. Everyone is self-conscious, and that's why God invented the dimmer switch. Wear sexy lingerie! Men are visual creatures, and the image of you in a teddy will linger long after this night. Speaking from past experience, test-drive the lingerie, especially if it has a lot of hooks. I had a particularly stressful experience with "thigh highs." Set the mood with candles, massage oil, condoms, and get rid of the kids. A quick note about condoms - use them no matter what your partner says. If he says he hasn't had sex in 20 years with anyone other than his wife, wear a condom anyway. If he says he was living in a monastery in Tibet, wear a condom anyway. Don't trust anyone until you see the lab report that says he is clean. A friend of mine found out the hard way when a guy didn't divulge that he had herpes.

Be honest with your partner about your fears and/or anxieties about sex. If you don't feel comfortable talking about this, don't have sex. You're not ready. Communication is the key to having great sex. You don't need to point out your C-section scars the first time, but you need to express any concerns that may prevent you from having an enjoyable experience. As your relationship progresses, you will need to feel comfortable enough to attempt different positions, role play or tell him/her what uniquely pleases you. This can only be done (unless he's psychic) if it's communicated. Please remember that things are different now than back in the hippie days. This means that you'll need to trim the hair on your private parts. If you've never done it, you may find that it's surprisingly erotic. Being clean and groomed will add to feeling sexy and confident.

Think about your sexual needs. Are you capable of having a "friend with benefits"?

Many newly single people go through a period of renewed adolescence. This can last anywhere from four months to 40 years. After being in a long-term relationship or marriage, being single can be lonely, and one way to comfort yourself is through physical affection – simply put, you're horny and you want to have sex. Being able to have sex with whomever you want is a major perk to being single. This sudden unleashing of sexual restrictions can be liberating as long as it's done safely. There are problems that can occur both physically and psychologically if you jump into sex without thinking of the consequences. Think about how you felt the first time you lost your virginity. A lot of the feelings of anxiety and excitement are similar when you pop your cherry the second time around. You may be more confident about sex now than at nineteen, but sex is still a very intimate activity, and your feelings may get hurt as a result. I found this newfound sexual freedom to be exciting but on a few occasions depressing. A "friend with benefits" is all that you may want or can handle if you're newly single. You may be so overwhelmed with your new life that anything more than a sexual relationship would be too complicated. If you have great sex with this person, you might end up fantasizing that it will turn into more. Friends with benefits could work, but you both need to be of a similar mindset. This is no easy feat, and communicating is key once again.

Realize the advantages and disadvantages of texting and sexting.

We didn't grow up texting. Texting is much easier than having to pick up the phone or have a discussion in person. It's also easier to be misunderstood, and the problem is that once the text is out there, you can't take it back. It sometimes ends up going to the wrong Adam or Kevin (oops). I've personally read and re-read a text several times trying to get to the deeper meaning, only to find out that there wasn't one.

Sexting takes it one step further. Sexting is sending naked pictures or writing provocative texts in emails or on cell phones. It can be a lot of fun, and it also can get you into a great deal of trouble. Sexting can give you a false sense of closeness, since it's easy to be brazen when you only have to press a few buttons. Be careful of what you send that can come back and bite you in the butt. If you send a nude picture and get into a fight with that person, you may find that photo on someone's Facebook wall. I've seen this happen on at least two occasions.

Close those eyes one more time, and envision the person with whom you'd want to ride off with into the sunset.

What does he look, sound, or act like? Now open your eyes. If that person isn't standing in front of you, it's because he doesn't exist. There is no perfect person out there. You need to come to the realization that the Prince isn't going to come riding in on a white horse and sweep you off your feet. You are going to have to compromise (but not settle) on what you want. If having great character is important, then you may not get the gorgeous multimillionaire. You may get the shorter-than-you'd-like sweetheart of a guy. On the other hand, you should never accept a man just because he has two arms, two legs and a penis.

Try to think outside the box. You may happen to fall in love with someone of a completely different religion, race, or age. Back to me: I'm currently dating a man who's years younger than me. This was NOT something I was actively seeking when we met. Try to be open to being with someone different with whom you really click and then go for it.

You can open your eyes now. It is time to begin your adventure the second time around. It's your life – don't wait to love it!

FIVE

....

WHEN WILL I FIND THE RIGHT ONE?

Age is not important unless you're a cheese.

-HELEN HAYES

Q: What advice do you have for women who are skeptical about finding love because of their age?

A: There is no timeline for love! It happens when it's supposed to happen. The most important thing for you is to find your passion and enjoy life to the fullest. Choose what is going to make YOU happy for the rest of your life regardless of whether or not a man (of any age) is going to be involved. Before entering into a relationship with anyone, you need to make yourself into the best person you can be, physically, mentally and spiritually. Why would you want a man who cares more about someone's age than the person inside? Men are attracted to independent, confident women, not needy, desperate girls!

Q: How do you handle all your past negative experiences about dating and relationships?

A: A good dose of self-exploration and some therapy by a professional therapist or qualified clergy member, not a girlfriend who will just tell you what she thinks you want to hear, will serve you well as you explore your singlehood. This will allow you to release a lot of past emotional baggage. Many women (and men) have fears of being alone and get sucked into a negative, "I'll never find anyone" state. You need to stay positive and good things will happen when you least expect them! On the practical side, you need to work out your body AND your mind. This will certainly help to increase your confidence and most of all, teach you to follow your gut instincts – they won't let you down!

Q: How do you handle honesty about yourself and your past in a new relationship?

A: Many interactions, first dates and relationships can be disappointing. It's up to you to share your feelings with someone with whom you might want a relationship. How? You can adopt the new COUGAR mentality. Remember that you'll need to be totally open, honest and confident if you want to move that relationship forward. He is LUCKY to have you, but if you withhold your feelings and don't communicate your needs, you will not get the respect that you deserve.

Q: What advice would you give a woman who thinks that sharing her feelings and emotions makes her seem clingy and needy?

A: It's a balance – you don't want to suffocate a guy, but you do need to let him know if you feel you aren't being respected or appreciated. As Tucker Max, author of "I Hope They Serve Beer in Hell" says, "Ladies, let me give you some advice. You can throw all your stupid fucking chick-lit, self-help, why-doesn't-he-love-me books out, because this is all you need to know: Men will treat you the way you let them. There is no such thing as 'deserving respect;' you get what you demand from people. If you demand respect, he will either respect you or he won't associate with you. It really is that simple!"

Q: Can you share your thoughts on chemistry in a relationship? Can it grow over time?

A: I'd be lying if I said chemistry doesn't matter. You feel that spark right at the beginning, and it could be based on looks, sense of humor or just a feeling. Sometimes a smell can be the most attractive thing about a man – you know what they say about pheromones. People can become much more attractive if they have a great personality that blossoms over time.

Q: What can you say to women who have the tendency to idealize men and/or overestimate his feelings for her?

A: This is a delicate subject not to be ignored! Guys who own their problems and seek help for them can be keepers. But those who are full of excuses or unresolved issues are going to be a bigger let down later on when those red flags rear their ugly heads. Better to get these issues out on the table right away so you don't imagine something that's just not there.

Q: What is your advice about when is the right time to bring sex into a relationship?

A: Have sex when it feels right. The right guy is going to want to continue seeing you regardless of spending time in the bedroom.

Q: Can you share your feelings on how honesty might negatively affect your chances for a long-term relationship?

A: I can't stress how important it is to be honest right from the beginning. That doesn't mean you need to bombard a guy on the first date about your unresolved issues, cheating, and other mistakes. But as soon as it makes sense, let him know who you are and who you have been. If he runs, better sooner than later. That having been said, all human beings have behaviors that have the possibility of turning off a potential mate. That doesn't mean, however, that those behaviors or habits can't be altered, especially if you are able to communicate how they make you feel. Some of them might be deal breakers, and only you will know if change is realistic. Don't ever think your man will just decide to change without guidance. Sometimes they can't, and it's probably better to know that upfront. Accepting bad behavior from the beginning and then expecting it to change later is not going to work. This goes along with faking an orgasm – don't EVER do it! Let your guy know what your expectations and needs are and then lead by example. If the guy really cares about you, he is going to want to please you and compromise about the things that aren't working for you. The Cougar would rather be alone than stuck with a smelly fish!!

Q: What advice do you have for women who are dealing with a man who suddenly pulls away or has inconsistent behavior?

A: Men can be unpredictable, especially early on in a relationship. If you feel you're on an emotional roller coaster, it may be time to step back and decide if this is how you want to live. Some men get cold feet and break up a seemingly good relationship due to a fear of intimacy. If this happens once and he returns (hopefully having seen a therapist), you may want to give it another go. If you're devastated and don't understand what happened, just assume that it's his loss. That doesn't mean guys deserve a "get out of jail" free pass just because they suffer from occasional cold feet. One time can be tolerated, after that, adios! If out-of-the-blue breakups occur in multiple relationships, seek help as to what you might be contributing to this pattern of behavior. Once again, instinct will serve you well.

Q: What are your three top relationship tips to offer single women looking for a long-term, committed relationship?

A: Be honest, confident, and allow your inner light to shine through. Be positive and don't "look" for a relationship, be "open" to one. Having a sign that says "Stage Five Clinger" on your forehead is a surefire way to send a date running for the hills. Give your boyfriend respect and expect to be treated the same way. Most important tip (okay, this is #4) – HAVE FUN!

SIX

....

THE SELFISH ORGASM

Sex pleasure in woman is a kind of magic spell; it demands complete abandon; if words or movements oppose the magic of caresses, the spell is broken.

-SIMONE DE BEAUVOIR

"Karen, how do I know if I've had an orgasm?" My friend Ronna asked me.

"Have you ever masturbated?"

"No, but I have great sex with my husband."

"*Ronna,*" I said, "*You need to have a SELFISH orgasm.*"

Ronna's expression was like a deer in headlights. I thought, **Is it possible that a 32-year-old woman had never masturbated and achieved an orgasm?**

Are there others out there with the same lack of orgasmic experience? This is a tragedy! Men talk about masturbating all the time. You hear male comedians constantly referring to "rubbing one out" or "whacking off" without a moment's hesitation.

Women tend to keep their masturbation hidden. I love nothing more than bringing up the subject with my friends. There are some who talk openly about their favorite vibrators, but there are others too mortified to broach the subject. I want to scream, "Women, come out of the closet!" (No pun intended.) **Orgasms deserve the same equality as equal pay.** It's the dawning of the selfish orgasm for women, and you don't want to miss it.

So what does it MEAN to have a selfish orgasm? It's about having a delicious, mindful orgasm without thinking about anyone else. Having an orgasm without worrying what your partner is thinking or feeling is liberating. If you're in charge of your orgasm, you can regulate the timing and intensity. You can use toys, read sexy books, or watch porn while enjoying a stress-free, purely self-absorbed experience.

Fantasizing plays a huge part in the buildup to an orgasm. It's a lot easier to focus on this alone, rather than simultaneously trying to balance the needs of your partner. Checking out your vagina in a mirror while playing with yourself is a huge turn-on as well as a learning experience. How will you know what really gets your motor going if you haven't tried out your vehicle first? You have the owner's manual and learning what makes you purr is an individual process.

Additionally, if you want to enjoy the same orgasmic bliss with a partner, you'll have to school him as to what works for you. Once you figure out those details for yourself, you can articulate them to him (or her). Even if you currently don't have a partner, it's all the more reason to keep your body sexually tuned up!

Having a selfish orgasm is giving yourself the pleasure that you deserve. It's time to enjoy the benefits of being a woman, so explore, enjoy and explode.

SEVEN

....

CHOOSE YOUR FACE OVER YOUR BUTT

I never worry about diets. The only carrots that interest me are the number you get in a diamond.

-MAE WEST

I had always agreed with my sorority sister's favorite saying, "You can never be too skinny or too rich." I rationalized that being uber rich might have its problems, but I would deal with them while traveling throughout the world on my yacht. However, as I passed my 40th birthday marker, I began to question, "Can you be too skinny?" I looked in the mirror and concluded that her theory on never being too thin had some serious draw-backs. Sure, when you're super skinny, you'll be able to fit into your bikini from 1975 and slide into your size two jeans with ease, but these advantages come at the expense of something far more valuable — YOUR FACE!

After a certain age, you will need to make THE CHOICE. What's more important... your face or your ass? After extensive personal research, I've determined that my face is by far the winner.

1) You can see it in your face.

Has this chain of events ever happened to you? You step on the bathroom scale, see a weight loss of a few pounds, leap in the air with excitement, go to the grocery store, bump into a friend and she exclaims, "Wow you lost weight, I see it in your face?" Your face is always the first place that looks thinner, not your thighs, waist or butt. Your mug looks longer, creases form on your cheeks, and the skin under your chin starts to sag. You appear older — not the look you were going for.

2) Big butts are in style.

We are now in the age of the Beyoncé and Kardashian butts. These two women have revolutionized the whole "Does my butt look fat?" question. People are even getting butt implants! This is life altering for those of us who've always tried to minimize their derriere. Thank you, Beyoncé for making it a plus to have a plus-sized prime beef rump roast.

3) Say no to bony butts.

Along with the aesthetic value of a bigger butt, it helps to have a little extra padding there if you happen to fall down. As we get older, a boney bum can turn into a broken tailbone if you happen to slip on some ice. A little cushioning provided by a few pounds can help soften the blow and save you a lot of physical therapy. Remember the "Charmin" commercials?

4) Fillers are painful.

Botox and other fillers for your face are costly and painful. Having a little fullness in the face gives a smoother look with fewer wrinkles. You can avoid the frequent trips to the dermatologist by eating that extra piece of pizza and letting your face enjoy the benefits.

5) Say no to plastic surgery.

To take it one step further, you'll be able to postpone a facelift or other surgical procedures that tighten your skin. You also won't walk around looking as if you are perpetually surprised or resemble Kim Novak at the 2014 Academy Awards. Going under the knife can be a costly and potentially life-threatening experience.

6) Your face is the most important part of your body.

Your face is what people look at 90% of the time. Who walks around backwards? As long as your job isn't a docent at the museum and you're not inclined to do the moonwalk, your face is what's seen the majority of the time. You'll want it to look as smooth and wrinkle free as possible.

7) Eating is a pleasurable experience. You will be able to enjoy a good meal with friends rather than splitting a side salad and drooling over everyone else's entree. What could be more frustrating than eating a few pieces of lettuce and a green bean while everyone is gobbling up their scrambled eggs and bacon? Your face will have a big smile on it when it's well nourished.

8) It takes too much time and energy to be on a diet. You won't have to plan your meals in advance and be in a constant state of hunger. Your face will not have a perpetual frown with worry lines from the stress of not eating enough green leafy vegetables and indulging in too many carbs. You can sleep comfortably and won't have nightmares about eating a piece of cheesecake.

9) Choosing your face will definitely help your mood. You won't be irritable and stressed about gaining a pound or two. People won't be bored listening to what your latest fad diet is and how much weight you've lost. You'll be a happier person — and so will they!

10) Having a flat ass doesn't help your sex life.
Your partner might hurt his hand giving a little love tap to your boney bum. Some men say, "The bigger the cushion, the better the pushin'." Yes, men seem to like a fuller bottom.

So, what's it going to be? Do you want to live your life, trying to look like a runway model with an eating disorder, or would you rather pinch a little more than an inch and enjoy your youthful plump face? The choice is yours! Don't forget what Sir Mix-a-Lot says, "I like big butts and I cannot lie."

EIGHT

....

LET'S REDEFINE THE WORD: C.O.U.G.A.R.

I've always been attracted to women who are assertive and have confidence - qualities older women possess. They've been on the Earth a little longer. They're more seasoned. They don't play games. They know what they want, and they're not afraid to tell you.

-TAYE DIGGS

Who was your favorite character on Sex and the City? Admit it, Carrie was sweet, but Samantha was fascinating. Samantha was hot! She dressed sexy, dated younger men, and wasn't afraid to shock the others with tales of her sexual exploits. Samantha took pride in her body and mind. She was financially independent, loved her job, passionate about her friends, and had a great sense of humor. Samantha was a Cougar!

I know a lot about Cougars because I'm a Cougar. My husband of 24 years was suddenly ripped from my life, and I became a widow at age 47. I was unprepared for my metamorphosis from kitten to Cougar, but everyone's journey is different. I'm currently in a committed relationship with a younger man, but that's a small part of my being a Cougar. In fact, I have redefined the term Cougar to mean a woman who is a: Confident, Older, Unique, Genuine, Assertive, and Racy. Any woman can possess these traits – married or single. We all have it within us, and I challenge you to release your inner Cougar!

A Cougar is **CONFIDENT!**

Confidence is the cornerstone of being a Cougar. A Cougar is confident on both physical and mental levels. She works out, eats healthy, and keeps her body fit. This doesn't mean that you need to have the perfect body to be a Cougar. Take the body you have and make it the best it can be. If you can't afford a gym, find ways to exercise at home. We realize that we have only one body, and although gravity is pulling it down, we continually strive to make it better. Wear makeup because there's no such thing as a natural beauty, color your hair, and accentuate the positives in the way you dress. If you have great boobs, wear low cut tops. If you like your butt, invest in a hot pair of jeans.

Your body language says EVERYTHING, so strut your stuff. Have you ever noticed that the most popular girl in high school wasn't necessarily the prettiest or had the best figure? She exuded self-confidence! Here's where the mental aspect to being a Cougar comes into play. Cougars don't worry about what "people" think about them. A Cougar knows who she is and what she wants to do with her life. If you follow what your gut is telling you, you will succeed. It's that simple. This applies to how you raise your family, deal with friends, and become independent of others. As you support yourself, your self-esteem rises immensely. Cougars have the inner strength to filter out the advice of judgmental "well meaning" friends and family. We go to therapists or meditate in order to clear our minds. Cougars work at keeping their bodies and minds in the best possible condition.

A Cougar is **OLDER** and proud to say it. As Samantha Jones states, "I'm 52, and I will rock this dress." Your wrinkles are your war wounds. You've had awesome experiences in your life: raised children, worked various jobs, traveled, and survived tragedies. Cougars have had the experience to know what's important in life. An older woman has had many great sexual experiences. You're like a fine wine or an ancient tree. You may have a few more aches and pains, and you may have to wear reading glasses, but you have wisdom that is invaluable. Being older and wiser makes us great mothers. We've taken care of ourselves and therefore we're able to impart our love and wisdom onto our kids. I have an incredibly open and honest relationship with my three children. If they want to talk about sex, drugs, or rock and roll, they know that I'm game. Who wouldn't want this relationship with a parent? The transformation into a fully actualized Cougar takes years. This is why you don't see too many Cougars under 40.

A Cougar is **UNIQUE**, and that's a good thing. If we were all the same, think how boring life would be. Cougars are women who at times can fit into the crowd, but it's not imperative to her existence. You are a snowflake, and no two are alike. As a Cougar, you'll want to dress, act, and experience life in your own special way. If you think you're different in a positive way, people will flock to you. Don't stifle your fun and vibrant personality to be like every other woman your age. Be a joyful, unique woman who speaks her mind. Some women lose their identity after they get married and have families. They become someone's wife or mother, and those wonderful independent women are somehow pushed into a corner. I quit my job when I had my first child, and followed the traditional role of mother and wife. I put my heart and soul into raising three kids and enjoyed my life for several decades focusing on everyone's dreams but my own. In speaking with many women who've gone through a divorce, a common theme they learned was, "Never lose YOURSELF." Having a career is liberating. It allows you the freedom to never be reliant on a man in order to live your life to the fullest. Date outside of your religion, race or economic level if you find that person fulfills your needs. Don't let the "Judgmental Judy"s deter you. If you want to date a younger guy because you have a younger spirit, don't worry about what people will think, just go for it.

A Cougar is **GENUINE** and doesn't try to be someone she's not. You shouldn't dress or act like the person your partner wants. You need to be real! I've seen some women try to be the prim and proper girlfriend or wife only to feel like a fraud. If you follow your gut, you'll know who you are and how to be yourself even if you're different than the people around you. Don't try to fit into a crowd that makes you feel inferior because you aren't like them. It's very freeing to be yourself. The alternative is to feel fake and pretentious. This ultimately causes negative, hostile resentment over time, and that's not very Cougar-like.

ASSERTIVE is a key component to being a true Cougar. If someone hurts you and you let him, you're teaching him that being harmful is ok. I wasn't always outspoken, in fact I was extremely shy. Somehow, I realized that this didn't get my needs met, and I began to speak up. Assertive is not aggressive! You don't want to hit someone with a stick instead of calmly articulating your thoughts as to why you won't accept poor behavior. As a Cougar, you're a role model to your family and friends. If you feel strongly about something, speak your mind and don't hold back. Being your own advocate is the best thing you can do for yourself. If you don't help yourself, who will? Men are definitely attracted to this strength. It's a turn-on. They prefer independent free thinkers rather than needy, insecure, non-challenging women.

Naturally a Cougar is **RACY**. Cougars love to express their sexuality. They're comfortable talking about sex. They realize the importance of sex and intimacy in a relationship. If you want to be thought of as a vibrant, sexy woman for life, then embrace that part of you. Men are attracted to women who exude confidence in their bodies and desires. Being racy in the bedroom will definitely enhance your sex life. Wearing racy clothing when it's appropriate is fun and keeps you from becoming old and matronly. Guys can usually spot a Cougar a mile away. They can tell that she's confident in her sexuality because of the way she walks, talks, and dresses.

Are you ready to become a confident, older, unique, genuine, assertive, and racy woman? Get your Cougar pride going and release that inner feline. The next time you're with your friends discussing who you identify with on *Sex and The City*, you know who to choose – Samantha.

NINE

....

DATING WIDOWS VS. DIVORCEES

Failures are infinitely more instructive than successes.

-GEORGE CLOONEY

Six months after my husband died, I decided to venture out into the singles world. I sauntered into a swanky downtown Chicago restaurant with a divorced female friend. She left me perched on a bar stool to go to the restroom. I stared at the glassware on the shelves behind the bar and a guy suddenly appeared. "So when did you get divorced?"

I replied, "I didn't get divorced."

He said, "Well where's your husband?"

Never one to pass up a good line, I said, "Six feet under."

That resulted in a jaw dropping, confused, uncomfortable, pitiful facial expression, as he stammered, "I'm so sorry."

I blurted out, "But I didn't kill him!"

This opened the door to a litany of questions: "Do you mind if I ask what happened? Do you have kids? Was that very difficult for you?"

"I'd rather not talk about it," I mumbled.

The next question was a shocker, "Do you mind if I ask you how long it has been since you've had sex?"

My response was - without missing a beat, "Twenty-four hours."

That interchange was my initiation into the "Planet Single Bar Hopping Phase." I later entered the "Planet Single Dating Phase." Here are 10 tips to understanding the differences in dating widows as opposed to divorcees:

1) Divorcees didn't have a happy marriage or they'd likely still be married. Widows had a happy marriage – or at least they only remember the happier times.

2) Divorcees have spouses who are regularly involved in their children's lives. The spouse helps with decisions about the kids; attends their sporting events, theater performances, and weddings. Widows don't have co-parents

to rely on, but also aren't required to listen to their spouse's opinions on child rearing.

3) Divorcees get a break from parenting if they have shared custody. Widows have a full-time parenting gig.

4) Divorcees may get some ongoing financial support for the children and/or alimony payments. Widows may have inherited life insurance, but it's typically a one-time payment.

5) Divorcees may have hostility towards the ex and perhaps the entire male population. Widows generally have a favorable opinion about the opposite sex.

6) Divorcees may feel relieved to be single again and eager to jump back into dating and sex. Widows may feel abandoned by the death of their spouse, and reluctant to try new relationships. They might feel guilty about being disloyal to the deceased if they date a new person.

7) Divorcees have to deal with an ex who may be a pain in the butt. The ex might stop by the house with little regard for boundaries. Widows don't come with the ex-factor baggage.

8) Divorcees may compare the new person with the ex. The new partner may feel the need to prove that he/she is different than the ex. Widows may reverently talk about the deceased to their new partners sometimes causing discomfort and insecurity.

9) Divorcees likely didn't have the best sex life towards the end of the marriage. They may be excited to be with someone who enjoys sex and wants to be inti-

mate again. Widows in happy marriages may have had an enjoyable sex life and realize the importance of sex in a relationship.

10) Divorcees frequently have had family and friends who sided with one spouse over the other. Widows' family and friends may be happy to include the new person into their lives or it may be hard for that guy/girl to walk in the shadow of the deceased.

Can widows be happy dating divorcees and vice versa? Absolutely, knowing the history of your partner's past is key to a successful future relationship.

TEN

....

THESE RED FLAGS ARE BASED ON TRUE STORIES!

Sometimes I wonder if men and women really suit each other. Perhaps they should live next door and just visit now and then.

-KATHARINE HEPBURN

You're officially single again. You're going to bars and men are starting to notice you. It's flattering, exciting and scary at the same time. A hot guy approaches and offers to buy you a drink. Your heart starts racing as you notice his sparkling eyes and wolf-like smile. The conversation flows and the chemistry is amazing. Could this be the next Mr. Right? It's possible — but be on high alert. Don't be snared by the seasoned hunter who's ready to pounce on some fresh new meat. Here are 10 traps (based on true stories) that should set off the newly single woman's fight or flight response:

Trap #1: That's not my wedding ring!

He's wearing a gold band on his fourth finger. You ask him point blank if he's married, which he emphatically denies. Upon further inquiry, you ask why he's wearing the ring. He reaches for his phone and shows you pictures of his "deceased" parents. He whispers, "This is all I have to remember my parents who were happily married for 50 years." You immediately feel guilty for mentioning the ring and are relieved when he changes the subject. It slips out later in conversation that he actually is married, and was hoping you'd "be cool" about it after getting to know him better. Lesson learned: If the tiger's got stripes, he's a tiger!

Trap #2: His credit cards have just expired.

You're having a great conversation with a cute guy at a restaurant bar. He offers to buy you a drink and you accept. The bartender asks if you'd like to start a tab. The generous man nods and proceeds to order some appetizers. You're having a great time talking to this entertaining guy until the bill arrives. He reaches for his wallet and mutters, "I'm so sorry, I just realized that my credit card expired and I'm low on cash. Do you think you can cover this? I'll get it next time!" Lesson learned: If the fox tricks you once, don't let him do it again.

Trap #3: He trash-talks his ex-wife.

You're standing in a crowded bar and a man initiates a conversation by asking how long you've been single. You proceed to tell him that it's only been a few months. He snorts, "I've been divorced for ten years, and it was all her fault. She's a "psycho." The name-calling continues until you finally find a way to exit. Lesson learned: A venomous snake isn't someone you want to tangle with.

Trap #4: He's had a few DUIs, so you'll need to drive.

You're having a great time partying with a man you met at the bar. When you're getting ready to leave, he asks if you'd like to go out with him the following evening. You agree and give him your phone number. He then drops the bomb, "Will you be able to pick me up?" You ask why and he explains, "I don't have a license right now, cause I had a few too many DUIs." Lesson learned: You don't want a drunken monkey on your back.

Trap #5: He hasn't spoken to his mother in years.

After ten minutes of talking about various subjects, you ask if he has a large family. He says he's an only child and that his father passed away. You remark, "You must be very close with your mother." He snaps, "I haven't talked to her in seven years, she's a witch." Lesson learned: If a cub doesn't love his mama bear, he won't treat you well.

Trap #6: He's married, but they haven't slept together in years.

After small talk, he admits to being married. "Our marriage has been on the rocks for years. We sleep in separate bedrooms. I can't even remember the last time we've had sex." The words free flow out of his mouth, and you wonder if what he's saying is really true. Lesson learned: Once a cheetah, always a cheetah.

Trap #7: He only talks about one subject — himself!

A man begins a conversation by telling you that he has a boat, two homes and a fancy sports car. He offers to take you on a vacation, since he has "timeshares everywhere." He pulls out pictures of his three daughters and regales you with stories as to how talented they are. After 20 minutes, you realize he hasn't asked you your name. Lesson learned: A gorilla beating his chest doesn't need a mate, he needs a mirror.

Trap #8: He's waiting for his inheritance to come through.

You're having a nice dialogue with a man. He's single, good-looking and personable. You tell him that you're in sales and inquire as to what he does for a living. He tells you that he works for his father. He proceeds to add, "I'm going to inherit a lot of money when he dies, and he's pretty old." Lesson learned: Don't date someone who has no loyalty.

Trap #9: His lies are revealed on the web.

A confident guy approaches your table. He sits and easily chats with your group of friends. He tells you that he's got a very cool job as an engineer with oilrigs, and he used to be a professional baseball player. The girls are all impressed and he asks for your number to meet up later for a drink. You exchange information, and he leaves. Your friend decides to Google his name and the first article that appears is a photo of his wife and two kids. Lesson learned: A coyote should cover his tracks.

Trap #10: He slept with every single woman in the neighborhood.

You're flattered when a sexy man begins to hit on you. He tells you he's attracted to your eyes and asks why he hasn't seen you out at the bars before. After you play a little game of "Who-you-know Geography," you realize he's the guy that went out with one of your friends and cheated on her with another. Lesson learned: A leopard doesn't change his spots.

Remember there are no hunting rules and regulations that men have to follow. If you're an innocent lamb, it's up to you to be prepared and on the lookout for the man-wolves who walk around in sheep's clothing.

ELEVEN

....

THE COUGAR EFFECT: WHY MEN BECOME ADDICTED

Be strong, believe in freedom and in God, love yourself, understand your sexuality, have a sense of humor, masturbate, don't judge people by their religion, color or sexual habits, love life and your family.

-MADONNA CICCONE

The younger man who has a sexual encounter with an older woman will remember it as some of the best sex of his life. The benefits will continue when the young man is ready for a relationship with a girl of his age. One result to having experienced sex with a Cougar is the attraction may end up becoming his "type." Once you're with a Cougar, you'll be hard-pressed to find a better tutor. This is called, "The Cougar Effect."

Here are ten reasons younger men say that their older lovers are sexually superior to their younger lovers:

1. It's a numbers game. The age of a Cougar age alone means many more years of experience with multiple partners. Before marriage, they may have had a few partners. After divorce, the notches on their bedposts may have gone up exponentially.

2. Older women have had lots of practice. Cougars have been in long-term relationships and marriages, which have provided years of sexual experience with one partner. Those memories are implanted into the older woman's brain, and whether good or bad, have shaped her sexual expertise.

3. Older women know what they want. Their self-awareness comes from years of experience and communicating with sexual partners. They've tried different positions, techniques, and fetishes. They've self-pleasured for many years, and aren't afraid of communicating the stuff that really gets them purring. If the woman doesn't know what she wants, it's hard for the man to figure it out. Cougars know exactly what they want and which buttons the guy needs to press.

4. **Cougars have learned what their men want.** They are eager to find out the specific desires of their current boyfriend. They've been taught by a variety of partners which positions and techniques turn men on. They ask questions and figure out what makes their man roar like the king of a lion's den. What they don't know, they will research in books, movies or on the Internet.

5. **The older woman enjoys sex as much as her younger male partner without hidden agendas.** They don't have any delusions that they are going to hook this man into marriage and/or start a family. This takes the pressure off a man who just wants to have fun without obligations. This stress relief is a major reason sex is great with an older woman who's not as needy or demanding.

6. **Older women realize the importance of sex in a relationship.** She may have been in a marriage where sex was withheld. She won't use sex as a bargaining chip or to try to get something materialistic from the younger man. Cougars know the psychological and physical benefits to regular sex.

7. **It is flattering to the younger man that a hot older woman finds him desirable.** It's a challenge to be with an attractive, sexy older lady who is physically fit

and keeps herself well groomed. She has the time to take care of herself since her children are older and more independent.

8. Older women enjoy teaching their eager younger students. They know when to be dominant and submissive. The man senses this knowledge and power, which is very stimulating. The older woman will bring books, lingerie, sex toys, candles and wine to set the mood.

9. Older women have confidence in their bodies and sexual prowess. This is a huge turn on for men who may have been with young girls who are just learning the ropes. The younger girls may be self-conscious and uncomfortable talking dirty in bed. Older women are spontaneous and comfortable being naked.

10. Older women aren't afraid of communicating. The younger man will know exactly where he stands with her. She won't play mind games with her younger man by not answering her phone. She will approach a man in a bar and not wait for him to make the first move. She will indicate what she wants from the relationship. She will openly share her sexual needs. She isn't worried about losing the man if she expresses herself.

TWELVE

....

TEN STEPS TO BECOMING A FLIRTING EXPERT

Some women flirt more with what they say, and some with what they do.

-ANNA HELD

"Why don't you come up and see me sometime?" Did Mae West brazenly utter those words? Gasp! Countless articles have been written on the rules of dating and she probably broke every one of those rules with that flirtatious question. Was she too bold? Was her attitude too aggressive? Doesn't she know how to play the game?

Flirting has somehow become wrong. It has become a lost art.

Why is mastering the skill of flirting a good thing if you're trying to get a date? The answer: Because men like confident women! This is the most common theme younger men say attracts them to older women. They're tired of always being the aggressors. They like women who are self-assured and know what they want. Flirting isn't easy but the rewards are great.

The act of flirting can dramatically increase your chances of getting asked out on a date. At the very least, if the guy you've flirted with isn't available, he'll still find you entertaining and remember you in the future.

I once flirted with a gorgeous guy who turned out to married. At the end of the evening, he asked if I'd consider dating his best friend who had just finalized his divorce. Flirting is a great opportunity to let your personality shine through. Here are ten steps to becoming an expert flirt:

1. Say hello to a stranger every day. This may seem easy, but it can be quite intimidating. The exercise of smiling, making eye contact and greeting a total stranger may seem completely foreign to someone who hasn't done this in the past. Ever since learning about "Stranger Danger" in grade school, we were taught not to make contact with strangers. The simple act of saying hello to new people will brighten your day and that of those whom you greet.

2. Give lots of compliments. Compliment a co-worker, friend, or stranger by saying something unexpected and nice. If you aren't able to leave your home, try saying a positive statement to someone on the phone. This is a good practice technique, which may yield a side benefit of getting your cell phone bill lowered since you were so sweet. Watch and listen to the reaction you receive from that person.

3. Introduce yourself to an unknown person. This can be anyone unfamiliar to you: your server at a restaurant, your grocery cashier, a bus driver. Make sure you smile and look the person right in the eye as you say, "Hi, my name is KarenLee. What's yours?" I know it sounds like a line from the musical *Gypsy*, but it made her a remarkably successful flirt, so give it a try.

4. Chat with a stranger. Go to a bar, restaurant, gym or any social gathering place and begin a conversation with someone you've never met. Talk for at least three minutes. The more comfortable you are with this step, the easier it is to start up a conversation with a man you are interested in getting to know.

5. You are now ready to approach someone you'd like to potentially date. This can take place anywhere: a bar, your favorite grocery store, the dog park, or the car wash. Be ready at all times so you don't kick yourself later about letting the guy get away. Once you've found your target, make friendly eye contact and give him a big smile. He's bound to respond positively.

6. Make your move! Walk up to that person and say something relevant about him or your surroundings. You can comment on the weather. You can discuss something on TV. You can even pretend to be interested in the sports team on his hat. Bring up any subject that will get his attention. Make sure to use great eye contact and give him your full attention.

Do not look at anyone else or pick up your cell phone. If he indicates disinterest by turning away or grunting a one-word answer, move on to the next guy. I once walked up to a group of guys in a club and boldly asked, "Which one of you guys want to dance with me?" I ended up dating the brave lad for over a year.

7. Keep the conversation light and flowing. Tell a joke and respond to his attempts at humor. Ask a question; then shut up and listen! This may seem obvious, but everyone likes to talk about his/herself or voice an opinion. If you listen intently and respond with a nod or smile, he'll feel special. If he shows you pictures of his kids or dog, you know you've captivated his interest. Those are a man's treasures, and he wouldn't bother bringing them out if he didn't care to impress you.

8. Make subtle body contact. Touch his arm, shoulder or hand. If you get really bold, you can brush your leg up against his. This tiny gesture will indicate you're interested in him as more than a friend. This will help keep you out of "The Friend Zone." If he returns the gesture, you're on the right path. (I wouldn't recommend grabbing his crotch — that's a bit TOO flirtatious.)

9. Keep the conversation short, sexy, and sweet. You want him to look forward to your next meeting. Find out if he's in a relationship. If he's available, tell him you need to leave but would love to see him again. If he hasn't asked for your number, think Mae West and say, "Here's my cell, call me sometime and we'll get together."

I once flirted with a guy at a bar who was waiting for his date to show up. I left him my card and offhandedly said, "If your date doesn't work out, give me a call." He called me the next morning, and we went out that evening. He said he was impressed with my self-confidence and couldn't wait to see me again.

10. Give him a sweet goodbye. Get up and shake his hand, give him a quick hug or, if you're comfortable, a light kiss on the cheek. Tell him how happy you are to have met him and say good-bye.

The art of flirting is not just about batting your eyelashes and tossing your hair. It's a skill that lets a man of any age know you're confident and he won't be rejected if he asks you out. If you wait for the guy to approach you, it may never happen. Mae West knew the secret to being an expert flirt, and now you do too. Go out and break some of those dating rules. In the words of Dolly Parton, (another woman who perfected the art of flirting), "I love to flirt, and I never met a man I didn't like."

THIRTEEN

....

THE FIRST KISS CAN DETERMINE EVERYTHING

Kiss me and you will see how important I am.

-SYLVIA PLATH

My mother always told me, "You have to kiss a lot of frogs before you find your prince." I thought she meant that it's a numbers game when it comes to finding the right man, but I now realize she meant the "kiss" part literally. You need to KISS a lot of men to find out if they are compatible smoochers before deciding on who should share your throne.

"Kissing is not just kissing. It is a major escalation or de-escalation point in a powerful process of mate choice," stated Helen Fisher, professor at Rutgers University.

That first kiss has always been the major factor in whether I went out with a guy again. Sometimes I'd expect an average kiss and be pleasantly surprised by his smooth delicious lip locking. Unfortunately, there were other times when I expected an amazing kiss that ended with me completely grossed out by his lack of passion or the clueless nature of how he kissed. Taking it one step further, you can determine how selfish/generous, passionate/dull, hostile/sweet, or humorous/boring a man is simply by the way he kisses. Does he tease you with his tongue or leave his lips locked on yours with the excitement of a soap dish?

My first experience with kissing was very anxiety provoking. I was eleven years old at a coed over night camp. One morning, I overheard some kids saying that we'd be playing Spin the Bottle that evening. I was excited at the prospect of my first kiss, until I realized that I had no idea how to kiss. I went into panic mode and decided I would need to practice on something. The only thing I found was a can of bug repellent. I frantically rolled my lips onto the can. Later that evening, we played the game and although the bottle landed on a guy with braces, I managed to have a fun time.

I have experienced my fair share of make-out sessions - the good, the bad, and the slobbery. I remember kissing my boyfriend, turned husband, on the floor in front of a burning fireplace. He stopped at one point to say, "I can kiss you for two weeks straight," and then we continued for at least another two hours. I have had instances where I couldn't stop kissing a guy even in public places like restaurants or taxis. Conversely, I've had horribly uncomfortable kissing sessions where I wasn't sure if he was giving me a kiss or swabbing my throat for a strep culture. Furthermore, I'm a firm believer that if the guy can't kiss, he probably can't do a lot of other important things in the bedroom.

If kissing is so important, why don't we get lessons on the art of kissing? Etched in my mind is an extremely sexy scene from television's Boston Legal, in which Julie Bowen teaches Mark Valley how to kiss. He wonders why he's able to get first dates, but never the second. She says, "There's a certain amount of gentility in kissing." He later says he doesn't like when a woman's tongue goes into his mouth. She responds, "This is why you're the worst kisser in the history of the planet."

Here are three scenarios of the importance of being a magnificent kisser: Someone fixes you up with a great guy. You meet at a local restaurant on the first date. It's an enjoyable evening and the guy is kind of cute. You don't notice any red flags. You leave the restaurant, and he walks you to your car. He leans in for a kiss.

He sensually presses his lips against yours and gently touches your tongue with his. He smells great and his breath tastes sweet. Your tongues do a little tango, and you feel a little jolt all the way down your body.

He holds your head between his hands and gives you a very passionate, sensual tasty kiss sliding his tongue into your mouth. You like his assertiveness, and you feel your heart race as you kiss him back with gusto.

He plunges his tongue into your mouth, swishes it around, drool drips from the sides of his mouth. His saliva gets all over your lips, as his teeth knock awkwardly against yours. You feel like a St. Bernard has just slobbered all over you.

What can you do to improve your kissing ability? Here's the most important tip to giving a kiss: It's a dance. Follow his lead, start slow and tune into the pace of your partner. Taste his tongue and lips as if you were savoring a piece of your favorite pie. Mimic his movements and mirror the way he touches your teeth and gums. Be playful, sensual, and romantic. If you put your tongue in his mouth, and he follows your lead, you're on the path to inheriting the throne. Is the first kiss really that important? You bet your regal lips it is!

FOURTEEN

....

RATE GREAT TO GET TO THE SECOND DATE

Self-confidence is the first requisite to great undertakings.

-SAMUEL JACKSON

You went on a first date and you didn't get asked out on the second. Let's figure out what happened by using a sliding scale. We're going to get two scores, and use them both to find the answer.

Part 1: Did you feel attractive? Did you wear something that you felt emphasized your assets and minimized your deficits? Using a scale of one to ten: from one = flabby, disgusting, ugly, Ursula the sea witch to ten = fit, curvy, smoking hot, Kim Kardashian, how did you feel walking out the door? If you "felt" like a five or above, you were on target. Notice I used the word "felt". You didn't need to wear $200 designer jeans to feel like a five. You didn't need to be a size four. You didn't need to have big perky boobs or an ass like a 21-year-old. You needed to have white teeth! (Sorry had to add that since it's a pet peeve of mine.) But seriously, you need to be comfortable in the body you have and feel sexy in your own skin. Wear clothes that make you feel great, and take some time to groom.

You can't start out a date feeling like a three because the date will sense it. Your date hopes for a nine, wants minimally a five, and certainly isn't going to ask a two out on a second date. Here's the secret to feeling like an eight before you leave your house for a first date: **It's 90% in your head and how you feel about yourself.** If you walk out the door and think that the extra ten pounds around your waist makes the difference between you being a two and a six, you have a choice to make. You can drag your two body back in the house, vow to stop eating for a month, and wait till you feel better about yourself before dating, or you can decide that you're curvy, your eyes sparkle, you have a great smile and strut that sexy booty into the car like the six you know you are.

Learn about body language. Here are some simple tips: Walk with your shoulders back and chest out.

When you enter a restaurant strut, don't hover like the freaking Hunchback of Notre Dame, walk in like you own the place! Slouching is not allowed and don't cross your arms over your chest. Don't pull your jacket over your blouse to hide whatever flab you think needs to be hidden. You don't want to look uncomfortable and insecure like you're trying to hide something when you should be flaunting those headlights. If you relax your arms and occasionally touch the person you're talking to, you will appear confident, open and attractive. If you're smiling with those pearly whites, your date will think he's in the presence of a winner. You are letting the date know how you rate and that he is with a cool, sexy person.

Part 2: How do you rate your personality on a scale from one to ten: from one = loser, sad, desperate, lonely, boring to ten = charming, witty, intelligent, happy, confident. If you're reading this article, you're at least a three since you have the ability to read and have a desire to improve yourself. Do you have interests or passions that make you unique? Did you laugh at anything I wrote so far? If you laughed you've already moved up to a four since you have a sense of humor. How's your listening ability? How much do you complain? If you are able to look on the bright side of things – think glass half full not half empty, your rating should be higher. Again, this is up to you to decide. If you feel miserable and that your life sucks, why the hell would that person want to see you again? That person doesn't want to be with a two when he's an eight. Think about your strengths. Do you love life? Are you a good person? What are three things that make you special? If you can't come up with something immediately that's ok, but give it some thought. If you're a gem of a person – a seven or an eight, and you come across as less than that, you're not going on that second date.

So there you have it. Take note of both those numbers, because they're equally important in getting you past date number one. If you think you're a double nine (everyone can improve a little), most likely your date will think the same, and if he doesn't see that, then someone else will.

FIFTEEN

....

GOOD RELATIONSHIPS TAKE THREE TRIMESTERS

Real magic in relationships means an absence of judgment of others.

-WAYNE DYER

Everyone knows it takes three trimesters to hear the first cries of a newborn baby. But did you know it takes three trimesters to give birth to a real solid relationship? Unfortunately, the timeframe is different. Good relationships don't necessarily take nine months; they may take nine years for your delivery.

First Trimester: Like the feelings you have when you find out you're pregnant; the initial surge of excitement when you connect with someone is intense and euphoric. The first few dates are heart pounding and your hormone switch flips into high gear. You can't wait to kiss that person at the end of a date. Your days are consumed by thoughts of the new guy. You think this person is too good to be true and red flags are quickly overlooked or minimized. For example: Did he cheat on an ex before getting divorced? You easily come up with a rationale, such as: his ex was a "psycho" or a "control freak." You explain the cheating with, "their marriage was on the rocks, and they were just staying together for the kids." You overlook annoying behaviors like his obnoxiously loud laugh, or the way he sends his food back every time you go out to dinner. The first trimester is a whirlwind of wild sex and passion that you can't imagine ever changing. Everything he does is <u>so</u> cute! You start to believe that this person could be "The One."

Second Trimester: The bun is cooking in the oven, and the reality of how life will change with your new baby is starting to hit home. You try not to go there, but you notice some flaws that seem to seep through that impenetrably perfect person. For example: His snoring didn't seem so loud at first, but now you're wondering if you'll need to take an Ambien every time you have a sleepover. You never realized that if he didn't make the plans for the evening, he would shut down <u>all</u> your ideas. You start to notice that what you thought was an iso-

lated incident of his losing his temper when a car cut
him off was really a horrible problem with road rage.
The little things that were no big deal in the first trimester have started to really bother you. This person has
begun to lose some footing on the pedestal that was
once a solid granite nonskid pillar. You mentally start
weighing the pros and cons of seeing him in the future.

Third Trimester: The little bundle of joy is about to
arrive, and you've accepted the fact that life is going to
be different. You begin to communicate and figure out
how to deal with the small issues that annoy you about
the other person. You focus on the positive aspects of
the man you're dating. For example: You sleep in separate bedrooms on the nights you know he drank a few
too many Johnnie Walkers and will snore louder than a
freight train. Conversely, there are character flaws that
are intolerable and can't be overlooked, such as his need
to humiliate you in public or the fact that he's physically
abusive. You try talking to him about your feelings, and
he storms out of the room and doesn't call you for days.
You find out that he cheated on you when he went ski-
ing in Aspen. This is the make-it-or-break-it part of a
couple and determines the future of the relationship.

Giving birth to a real relationship is not easy and un-
like the inevitability of a baby, you may decide to break
up. It can be a stressful, uncomfortable, bumpy road, just
like going through the aches and pains of carrying a baby. Is it worth it? Absolutely–everyone wants to find

"The One." You just need to go through all three trimesters until you feel that first slap on the tush.

SIXTEEN

....

WHISPERING ABOUT OF FIFTY SHADES OF GREY

To talk about adults without talking about their sex drives is like talking about a window without glass.

-GRACE METALIOUS

I'm reading *Fifty Shades of Grey*, whispered the blushing 60ish woman waiting for her nails to dry at the salon. "What's it about?" I asked. "It's about a girl with an older guy who's into bondage and other kinds of S and M sex," she replied. "Sounds like my kind of book," I answered as I whipped out my phone to make a note of it.

Shortly after that, I began hearing my friends discussing the book too. My friend Beth downloaded it on her Kindle and began reading it on an airplane. She said she was so nervous the person next to her could see the large print that she kept her arm covering it the entire trip. My friends' husbands and boyfriends all claimed not to have read the books but somehow were able to discuss certain explicit scenes in graphic detail. Everyone started to buzz about the books – mothers were sharing books with their daughters. My 80-year-old mother-in-law read the entire trilogy. The president of our temple brought it up in his appeal for funds stating, "We spend money on things like, *Fifty Shades of Grey*, which I'm certain every man in this room feels is money well spent."

What took women so long to start talking about their fantasies and kinky desires? Guys have no problem talking about how they regularly masturbate or how they fantasize about porn stars. I have always been comfortable talking about sex with practically everyone – except my parents. I remember getting my first vibrator back in college. I proudly showed my sorority sisters the pointy nose and little rabbit ears on my pink vibrating toy. I found tremendous pleasure reading books written by authors like Nancy Friday about women's sexual fantasies. I gave copies to my close friends for holiday gifts a few years back, and although they rolled their eyes at me, I know they read them cover-to-cover. Sex is fun, and talking about it is fun, too. It's a lot more entertaining than discussing news, weather or sports. One of the main causes of divorce is sexual incompatibility. The first step to solving this problem is to talk about it.

People are afraid to talk about sex and what they want from their partners. I'm here to say, TALK ABOUT SEX! Bring it up at when you go out with another couple for dinner. Ask them if they watch porn together. They may be shocked to hear that you tried it, but later they may decide to give it a whirl. If something worked for you such as using a small bullet vibrator during sex, why keep it a secret? Let's keep the *Fifty Shades* revolution rolling and talk about sex. It's not a shady subject anymore!

SEVENTEEN

....

PUPPIES AND MEN DON'T HAVE ESP

We need men and women to sit down and talk to each other about sex honestly and openly. That would help us fight AIDS so immediately. But our lack of communication is hugely problematic.

-EMMA THOMPSON

Just like with Pavlov's method of ringing a bell and getting a dog to start salivating, it's that simple to train your man to get your juices flowing. You'd never expect a new puppy to understand basic commands like sit, stay, and don't chew a Jimmy Choo shoe, so why would you expect your new partner to know what he's supposed to be doing in bed? I don't care how much experience your new lover had with his ex-wife of 25 years. He may have figured out what made her moist when he made love to her, but that doesn't mean it'll turn you on. Let's go over a basic tenet of behavior modification, which is the act of creating change in someone's actions by reinforcing the positives and punishing the negatives. In other words, giving your doggie a treat when he pees outside, and scolding him for pooping on your new rug. Now I'm not saying that you should give your man a bone (even though he probably will have one) when he licks your ear and plays with your nipples, but telling him that it turns you on lets him know that he's on the right track. I don't suggest yelling at him if you hate when he nibbles on your ear. A gentle whisper of "I'm not digging the bite marks" will do the trick. The most extreme example of poor training of your lover would be to fake an orgasm. Whatever he is attempting to do down there that doesn't excite you, like blowing on your clitoris or spanking your butt, needs to be addressed. You mustn't positively reinforce it by screaming out how you just had the most intense orgasm. He'll think he knows the secret to getting you off, and that the next time he does those things, you'll have a mind-blowing orgasm. He needs training and you're the only one who has the owner's manual on what makes you tick. Most importantly, you need to know how to make yourself have orgasms. You are the only one who knows if you need gentle circular motions on your clitoris and/or nipple pinching. There's a certain amount of trial and error that needs to occur, and one person's pleasure is another person's pain. You may want to use a vibrator while he licks your clitoris, and he may have never turned one on. Communicate your needs – he's not a mind reader. When he gets it right, praise him. You're sure to get a good response. Remember – there are no bad dogs, just bad trainers. Dogs want to please, and so do lovers.

EIGHTEEN

....

RELEASE YOUR INNER STRIPPER

It's been so long since I've had sex, I've forgotten who ties up whom.

-JOAN RIVERS

Yes, this means you! I don't care if you're married, single or something in between. It doesn't matter if your butt looks more like Roseanne Barr's than Kim Kardashian's. Stripping does not mean pole dancing. I've taken a pole dancing class, and you need to be part lemur to be able to climb a pole. Think Marilyn Monroe meets Madonna. It means taking off your clothes in a seductive manner with candlelight and sensual music in front of your man.

Stripping will boost your confidence and make you feel sexy. After you try this, your guy may be in favor of throwing a few dollar bills your way. Why do you think strip clubs are popular? If you ever went to one you'd realize the following: the girls are usually not good dancers, they don't have great bodies, and they aren't drop dead gorgeous. They have <u>confidence,</u> or they're very good at acting like they do! Men pay ridiculous amounts of money to see women remove cheap night-gowns and pretend they're interested in the poor girls. It's a huge turn on for a man to think he's getting a per-sonalized show – even if it's your guy who's in his Hanes boxers watching a Bears game. It makes you feel like you're hot, even if you haven't lost those ten pounds on Jenny Craig.

You need to do a little preparation when creating a bedroom/strip club. No - you don't need to install a pole in your bedroom. Start by digging out the pink sequined lingerie you bought on an impulse back in '98. I highly advise trying on the more complicated stuff in advance, since they may require a PHD in lingerie engineering. I found out the hard way, when I told my man to sit back while I bolted into the bathroom to slip into something sexy. I pulled the nylons over my thighs, slipped on a black bustier with 125 hooks, attempted to clip the four dangling ribbons onto the nylons, and failed to get one to stay attached. After 20 minutes of sweating, swearing, and breaking a fingernail, I waltzed back in the room looking like a disheveled mess. Consequently, I'm partial to assembling all clothing under a silky robe in advance. Make sure that you wear high heels. Don't worry, stripping doesn't require much moving around – trust me, I can barely walk in gym shoes. A little alcohol is good to relax you and free your inhibitions. Note the word "little." Translation: Don't get sloppy drunk because there's nothing worse then rolling your ankle, screaming obscenities, and waking the kids when you're trying to be seductive.

Lighting is also an important component. You never see a brightly lit strip club. My favorite line as I've gotten older is, "Darkness is my friend." Who doesn't have a little extra flab around their waist? Nothing works better than candlelight and a dimmed lamp when it comes to removing the signs of gravity on your body. Here's where the little insecure person in you is saying, "I have too much hanging here," or "I'd look stupid if I put on crotch-less panties." No you won't! You'll look great since it's dark and he can barely make out more than your silhouette. Now that you've got his attention, he'll be zeroing in on the mountains and the molehill.

Music is one of the most essential elements in creating the atmosphere needed for stripping. You don't hear Jimmy Kimmel doing his monologue in a club. I have my favorite stripper songs. Try Christina Aguilera's, "Nasty Naughty Boy" – the lyrics are very explicit.

Here is the play-by-play as to how to strip once the mood is set. Tell him you've got a surprise for him, but he'll need to close his eyes. If you're sparking his interest, but he is engrossed in the 7th inning of the Dodgers game, grab the remote, turn down the lights and press play on your boom box. Start by slowly strutting by him in your robe and letting the tie come loose. Tease him by running your finger down his leg and then backing away towards the wall. You may want to fantasize and close your eyes. Imagine you're in a room full of leering men and you're on stage as the star attraction. Press your back against the wall and squat down. As you rise up, open your robe so he gets a glimpse of the teddy. Prance around the bed and let the robe fall to the floor. Bend over him and let him inhale your perfume while you brush your hair against his face. Don't let him touch you. If you know the words to the song, sing along and tell him he's naughty for trying to grab you. By mid song remove your shoes and pull a strap off your shoulder. Lift one leg onto the bed and rub your body luxuriously. He may get over zealous and try speeding up the process by grabbing you, but hold your ground. Be playful and tell him to back off or you're sending in "Bruce the Bouncer" to toss his ass in the alley. Keep taunting him by rubbing your body on his and then backing off.

Towards the end of the song, remove your gown and keep your panties on. Get completely naked and climb on top of your eager partner. The next part is obvious, but I suggest continuing the role-playing to add variety to your lovemaking. Releasing the inner stripper in you is erotic and will bring a higher level of excitement to your sex life. Try it and as Madonna says, "Express yourself."

NINETEEN

····································

A COUGAR'S COMMITTED RELATIONSHIP

Love is like a virus, it can happen to anybody at any time.

-MAYA ANGELOU

I'm a Cougar. I'm also a widow. I was happily married to my husband, who was only a year older than me, and I wasn't aware that I had the "Cougar gene" in me until his death. After an intense period of mourning, I decided I needed male companionship, but wasn't ready to jump into a "serious" relationship. The term "Cougar" implies an older woman on the prowl for her prey - a "cub" or much younger man. I wasn't "on the prowl;" in fact, the young men pursued me. Although it was fun, I was completely unprepared for the flirting and aggressive questions that I encountered from men in their twenties and thirties, such as, "Have you ever done anal?" or "Have you ever been with another girl?" I had been in the "married" world most of my adult life, and never went through the dating scene. I have to admit, it was very flattering to be "hit on" by younger men. My daughter – age 22 at the time - informed me that an older man pursuing a girl in her twenties is considered "creepy." Conversely, there seems to be an unwritten code in the 21st century that promotes younger men being with older women. These young cubs had confidence, a full head of hair, muscular bodies, and dressed well.

At clubs, they bought us drinks and offered us seats at their VIP tables with bottle service. In one instance, a wealthy younger man who was interested in me actually paid a bouncer to keep annoying guys away from one of my friends. I was initially very naïve and didn't realize that you don't give your cell phone number to every guy who asked, because you'll get texted or called at four in the morning. On more than one occasion, a guy would call asking intrusive questions about my sexual fantasies or describe in a text how great sex would be with him. Guys would beg me to send naked photos (I never did), or occasionally texted unsolicited pictures of their proudly displayed penises.

Why would a guy in his late 20's or early 30's want someone who's older with three kids and stretch marks? Why not choose the younger nubile bodies of girls their age? I asked a few of my younger men what their reasons were, and they'd say, "Older women are hot." My guess is that they were attracted to my confidence, and the lack of pressure that I placed on them to be involved in a relationship. I didn't want to get married, I didn't want their money, and I certainly didn't want to have their babies. All I wanted was to have fun. Knowing that these were not going to be long-term relationships made it simple, and enjoyable at a time when my life was frequently unstable.

Going out with men my age was a different ballgame. Often this required me to listen to stories of wicked exes and the massive amounts of money they lost paying alimony and child support. Many of the guys had negative feeling towards women after being in failed marriages. Additionally, keeping in shape and being well groomed didn't seem to be a high priority for many older gents. There weren't a lot of widowers in their 40's, so most available men are either divorced or have never been married. To summarize, I found younger guys to be more desirable. They hadn't been married and had more positive, untainted views of women than their older divorced male counterparts.

This was my life as an "untamed" Cougar from Chicago until I met Steve. This tall, handsome, 33-year-old man wasn't looking to be involved in a relationship and neither was I. Our worlds collided on February 29, 2008 - a leap year, when my friend Susie and I crashed Steve's company's private party at "The Pink Elephant" in New York City. We were only in New York for one night, and what began as idle flirting turned into an intense attraction.

Neither of us could have predicted that our long distance relationship would survive the many obstacles ahead. Steve's devotion to me and his strong character are what attracted me to him. He's told me on more than one occasion that what he loves most about me is my upbeat personality. We thoroughly enjoy each other's company and respect one another. Age is only a number in our eyes.

Are there challenges due to big age differences? Yes! I think a main issue can be is if a couple's life goals are different. Thankfully, we seem to want the same things. In our case, I didn't want any more children, and I made that clear from day one. Steve has stated that having children wasn't a deal breaker for him. He's always put my three children's needs before his own, and that generosity of spirit is another of his endearing qualities.

We have gone through different life passages, and we're aware that we'll need to continually address this together as a team. We enjoy many similar interests such as music, comedy, and travel.

Introducing a much younger man as your boyfriend was no easy task. For instance, when men of my age found out that I was dating Steve, some sort of macho/defensive armor arose and remarks such as; "Are you going to babysit him?" or "Do you change his diapers?" were not uncommon. Women sometimes were equally rude, and called him my "Boy Toy." My parents were concerned that he would leave me when I started "looking old." His parents initially had no desire to meet me since I wouldn't be producing a grandchild. Over the years, our family and friends have witnessed our love and devotion and now accept and appreciate us as a committed couple.

There's a 50% divorce rate in the United States, and no guarantees that any relationship will last. For the past seven years, we've overcome two huge obstacles; long distance and a large age gap, and this in itself would indicate the  strength of our relationship. Is he going to leave me when I "look old"? He's probably no more likely to leave me than any same-aged man would leave a partner if she "looked old." Do we argue and have normal relationship problems just like any other couple? Of COURSE! Will I miss out on "the golden years" when my age group retires, and Steve is at the height of his career? My answer: He'll keep me young! Steve explained it best once when a friend taunted him about being with me. The friend asked, "Steve, why would you want to be with an old lady?" He replied, "Karen has a young spirit and I'm attracted to that." Will he resent me for not having his child? Again Steve said it best, "If I'm having as much fun with Karen in ten years as I do now, then all the sacrifices will be worth it."

ABOUT THE AUTHOR

KARENLEE POTER currently hosts an Internet talk show, The KarenLee Poter Show, and blogs about dating, sex, love and everything in between. Poter created the show after she became a widow. No topic is off limits as she shares personal anecdotes and opinions through witty vlogs and comedic shorts about her life as a "Cougar," which she has redefined as a Confident, Older, Unique, Genuine, Assertive, and Racy woman. Poter is also an expert in large age gap relationships, as she's been in a committed relationship for the past seven years with a man many years her junior. The KarenLee Poter show commands a worldwide audience, receiving nearly 100,000 views per month, and KarenLee's writing has been featured on multiple blog sites. She's a Chicago-based mother of three and has a Master's Degree in Social Work from the University of Illinois.

CPSIA information can be obtained at www.ICGtesting.com
Printed in the USA
LVOW06s1458060815

449113LV00019B/763/P